Kingdom Principles
For Effective Living

Ideal for Christian Growth

GILBERT COLEMAN

GILBERT COLEMAN

Kingdom Principles

For Effective Living

Ideal for Christian Growth

Hollis Media Group
Publisher

GILBERT COLEMAN

ISBN-13: 978-1539841135

ISBN-10: 1539841138

This book was printed in the United States of America.

To order additional copies contact the Publisher:

www.hollismedia.net

©2016

GILBERT COLEMAN

Table of Contents

DEDICATION   9
FOREWORD   11
INTRODUCTION   13
CHAPTER 1 Christians Struggle with Balancing Principles
                                                                 17
CHAPTER 2 In God We Doubt   23
CHAPTER 3 No More Crumbs   35
CHAPTER 4 Perfecting Our Love Walk   43
CHAPTER 5 The Importance of a Father   55
CHAPTER 6 The Responsibility of Leaders   65
CHAPTER 7 The Revelation of the Church   75
CHAPTER 8 The True Source of Strength   87
CHAPTER 9 When Mary Shows Up   95
About the Author   102

Tap the power within

DEDICATION

I want to first thank Almighty God for calling me to be a vessel for Him to carry the great treasure of His Word. Also, I am blessed to have my wife Debi by my side who understands the call of God on my life and releases me to be free to answer His call.

To one of the greatest families on earth, my children and grandchildren that are a constant support to me, and my Mom who saw God's hand on me at an early age and continued to pray for me, I love you all without measure. Lastly, I'm thankful for the many people the Lord has blessed me to minister to, who at one time or another have let me know that a message I taught helped them through challenging and difficult areas in their life.

GILBERT COLEMAN

FOREWORD

Although the world may be in a constant state of flux, chaos and disorder, Apostle Gilbert Coleman cuts away the fat of matters and gets to the meat, focusing on eternal, foundational principles. His thoughtful, introspective look at the kingdom of God is done with surgical precision and accuracy as he opens the scriptures in a most practical way.

Apostle Coleman turns our collective attention inward as he exhumes the ancient remains of a holy nation lost to implosion over millenniums. The kingdom of God has truly suffered violence, and what Apostle Coleman reveals, without embarking upon an exhaustive treatise, is the children of God are being called back to a state of awareness and consciousness of our responsibility to realign with our royal and divine pedigree. His words and ideas smack of revolutionary radicalism, as you will sense no blame for the world. All we get here is fresh perspective on personal ownership of the onus to become agents of change.

As readers, we are challenged to take an honest look at our understanding of and personal propensities towards love, our expressions of the spirit of love and our inescapable roles as kingdom ambassadors, called upon to show compassion for our fellow man. We are reminded that love is the quintessential factor for which we are to be known.

We are also compelled to adjust our perspective and attitudes towards the responsibilities of leadership. Apostle Coleman calls upon every reader to embrace the purpose for leadership, not merely the rewards. He calls on us to prefer responsibility for others, not power to Lord over them. Then, he clearly identifies the qualities of kingdom leadership and the reintroduction of reverence and honor, which seem to be lost disciplines among the people of God in this age of post-modernity.

This book is most necessary, in this age, to snap the children of the kingdom back to our Lord's grid of divine order, biblical adherence, and spiritual purity. I perceive this book will serve as a great reference, meant to be read numerous times, for those intending to be, do and have all to which heirs have access as beneficiaries of the most high God through Christ Jesus. — Rashiid K. Coleman

INTRODUCTION

For many years now the lack of emphasis on personal knowledge of God's word has impeded the forward progress and momentum of the church. Many believers are excited and exuberant over the proclamation of the word by their favorite preacher, and even take hordes of notes, but fail miserably in making swift application of what they hear. The Bible says of itself "That faith comes by hearing, and hearing by the word of God!" Our heart's desire should be to grow in the grace and knowledge of God's word and to become effective witnesses in the world.

The book that you hold in your hand is a small portion of what the Lord has shared with me over the last 34 years, that has brought great delight, strength, and joy to my life, and has made me into the man that I am today. It is imperative that each of us finds ourselves in His word daily if we intend to properly chart the course of life. In particular, every leader must realize that to effectively lead others you must first be led. No man or woman can lead others if they don't know what it means to be a follower.

The pages following will give you a brief understanding of what the Lord was saying to me to say to others at certain intervals in my journey. It has always been important to me to insure the fact that the word spoke to me first before I ministered to others. For me, there was no way that the word would minister to those I spoke to if it didn't first speak to, and then, bring conviction to my own life.

It also has been amazing to see how the Lord could give me something that was tailor made for a particular congregation or situation, and have the people respond to the supernatural power of God that loved them so much He sent a word to help them through their circumstances.

Unfortunately, there are many people that have made preachers and preaching iconic, thus, removing God from the equation and somehow replacing Him with a man or woman that is just as fallible as they are. The sole objective of every believer is to internalize the word so that it might conform us into a mature "man", and bring us to the stature of the fullness of Christ. The people of the world are hurting and they are desperate for answers. At present we are looking at a world that is filled with chaos and confusion; undoubtedly the Bible holds the key to unlock the untold potential and possibilities that lie within each of us, and to rid anyone of the nagging and gnawing internal inadequacies that hinder us from fulfilling destiny.

I don't profess to have all of the answers, but, I do know for certain that the word of God time and time again has provided the stability and security that I needed in any and every situation. It is my prayer that what you will read in these pages will bring you the comfort, consolation, strength, and power that it has provided for me over all the years of my life. Life's circumstances will at times want to suggest alternative sources for strength, but NOTHING will ever compare to God's holy word!!

"Your word is a lamp unto my feet and a light unto my pathway". Ps 119:105

Gilbert Coleman

CHAPTER 1
Christians Struggle with Balancing Principles

We are not to be swayed (convinced to move away from the foundational truths) - scripture forewarns of ideologies shaping the behavior of many that they would turn away from the "Living God" to adhere to seducing doctrine of devils and following their own heart.

We were not called to blend our faith, Believers are set apart to demonstrate their faith in the midst of darkness (which means, with the light of the WORD), we must stand up and stand out.

When we try to be relevant for the times and fail to adhere to what God wants accomplished, we become slaves to a subculture of ideology which is shifting.

Believers will be Ostracized, not invited to many events but we will have to settle that our position to live a full life with the internal peace of God or with a model that deteriorates because the foundation is not solid and supported by God principals.

Heaven is in me. We suffer for this but we must not be weary.

The art of creating and maintaining balance requires absolute resolution, and should be a paramount goal for every person; whether in business, a personal relationship or just casually mingling with friends, family and neighbors. It's imperative that we learn to press PAUSE and assess where we are and how we are utilizing our time and talent – every day matters.

Our ingesting of ideologies and labeling of positions (whether one is liberal or conservative) Baptist, Catholic or Pentecostal that we adhere to, becomes toxic to our relationship with God when our applications are not balanced by and with the word of God. Accuracy of Scripture is the only barometer that will keep one from falling into divers temptations, or deceived by seducing doctrines developed for the sole purpose to erode one's spirituality and contaminate the plan of God for your life.

Wherefore, we cannot overlook the derision many are living in---having eyes to see but unable to decipher evil before them; ears to hear, but is deaf to the cry of the Spirit to come back; being inundated with busyness, increasing in intellect, and yet, still fumbling in darkness searching for a positive path to provide harmony. Outside the will of God, our attempts to create what is considered a productive, more lucrative path is futile... especially if we don't understand that everything on earth is a loan. We came with nothing and we take nothing with us.

Commentary:

Herein is the struggle and conundrum for most believers; the pursuit to be relevant (modern---forward thinking, not antiquated or showing the appearance of being judgmental) cannot be perpetuated by enactment of a diluted approach to a timeless treasure (unwavering principle) called "holiness"- which explicitly means set apart for use. Yes, we are in the world and cannot escape being confronted by those who support what is deemed in their eyes as "progressive change," but the very applications are in opposition to Scripture. As well as increasing systemic pressure and discrimination against religious liberties. Notwithstanding, to every Believer it is given or required that we understand the seasons and times, and then know what to do. There is no excuse to be without answers… for it is the privilege we share as children of God that gives us a tactical advantage; he has made known the mysteries of the gospel, which are not governed by societal trends. Nor are Godly principles defined by legislative processes or eroded by someone's lack of faith because of the failure of a local church administration in their time of need.

Everything about God and his principles for living cannot vacillate from the original intent. They are exact, resolute and enforced, and speaks volumes of the original intent of God that Believers are to be living examples in the faith. Everything must be put in perspective…

Regardless of public scrutiny, it is required that we prove ourselves before God, being of sound mind, taught in scripture (our foundation), and to be a witness to all nations. There is no hiding place to blend and fake or live incognito, to do so dishonors God and demonstrate that we are ashamed of him. And if we deny him, he will raise up a testament of his power and presence because he cannot deny himself. We must honor God in every arena thus, fulfilling the very purpose for which we are called, to be a light on a hill; he only sends light where there is darkness and whole-heartedly upholds his purpose after the counsel of his own will that is independent of personal opinions and is final.

So, let us be encouraged and look to the author and finisher of our faith, Jesus Christ, and process our soul salvation in reverence and with intent to please him who has called us to live according to his glorious will.

CHAPTER 2
In God We Doubt
Lk 12: 16-21

Numerous Christians live a fear based life that prevents them from rising above their circumstances in their thought life. Ps 91: 5-9 You shall not be afraid of the terror by night, nor of the arrow that flies by day, nor of the pestilence that walks in darkness, nor of the destruction that lays waste at noonday. A thousand may fall at your side, and ten thousand at your right hand; but it shall not come near you. Only with your eyes shall you look, and see the reward of the wicked. Because you have made the Lord, who is my refuge, even the Highest, your dwelling place.

We are not always as cognizant as we should be of how we are influenced by the society around us more than we would want to believe. Deut 6: 10-15 So it shall be when the Lord your God brings you into the land of which He swore to your fathers, to Abraham, Isaac, and Jacob, to give you large and beautiful cities which you did not build, houses full of all good things, which you did not fill, hewn-out wells which you did not dig, vineyards and olive trees which you did not plant – when you have eaten and are full – then beware, lest you forget the Lord who brought you out of the land of Egypt, from the house of bondage. You shall fear the Lord your God and serve Him, and shall take oaths in His name. You shall not go after other gods, the gods of the people who are all around you (for the Lord your God is a jealous God among you), lest the anger of the Lord your God be aroused against you and destroy you from the face of the earth.

We live in an elitist society, who with their money, control the culture and its thinking. (Prov 22: 7) The rich rules over the poor, and the borrower is servant to the lender.

The lack of a Kingdom mentality has submerged us into a life of materialism.

Meditating on information that is contrary to God's word will cause us to create an environment of worry and doubt. (Mt 6: 25-27; 31-34) Therefore, I say to you, do not worry about your life, what you will eat or what you will drink; nor about your body, what you will put on. Is not life more than food and the body more than clothing? Look at the birds of the air, for they neither sow nor reap or gather into barns; yet your heavenly Father feeds them. Are you of not more value than they? Which of you by worrying can add one cubit to his stature? Therefore, do not worry, saying, what shall we eat? Or what shall we drink? Or what shall we wear? For after all these things the Gentiles seek. But seek first the Kingdom of God and His righteousness and all these things shall be added to you. Therefore, do not worry about tomorrow, for tomorrow will worry about its own things. Sufficient for the day is its own trouble.

The Lord has given us immutable laws designed to afford us everything He has promised to us in covenant. (Isa 14: 24) The Lord of hosts has sworn, saying, surely as I have thought, so it shall come to pass, and as I have purposed, so it shall stand.

A true believer understands that their concentration cannot be on themselves, but focused on the things of God. (Ps 36: 7-9) How precious is your lovingkindness, O God! Therefore, the children of men put their trust under the shadow of Your wings. They are abundantly satisfied with the fullness of Your house, and You give them drink from the river of Your pleasures. For with You is the fountain of life: in Your light, we see light.

One of our greatest challenges is that we don't understand the system the Lord has put in place to see His people prosper. (Eccl 2: 26) For God gives wisdom and knowledge and joy to a man who is good in His sight; but to the sinner He gives the work of gathering and collecting, that he may give to him who is good before God. This also is vanity and grasping for the wind.

Commentary:

The positive vantage point every believer should keep at the apex of their consciousness is "We are covered." This should be the mantra and battle cry of every born-again person. No matter what is thrown at you "if God is for you, who or what, can be against a child of God?" He has power to prorate your elevation, that which would naturally take decades to achieve, He can give the harvest in ONE season if we believe. It is because of the blood-covenant God protects the purpose for which you are called from destruction and will block external plots to overtake you that could deteriorate your destiny. If we submit to him He will keep that which is committed to his trust. A promise that should embolden the profession of our faith where we extract through the spirit realm those things that have been altered, raise our expectation, and launch an offensive stance against every demonic scheme as spiritual warriors and kingdom possessors simply because we have authority to do so.

Although in Scripture, it is apparent various forms of hardship comes to the life of the believer, however, our solace or comfort is in knowing we have an immutable word spoken over our life that must fulfill its mission. The word cannot return to God void or unaccomplished.

Therefore, peripheral concerns regarding materialism should not preoccupy our days nor annul our internal worship of who God is. Provision will be made because of your connection to the provider.

As we grow in Him, we learn to get better at living by deciding to surrender daily to the will of the father specifically in difficult periods. Whereas we strive to keep the biorhythm of praise pouring forth; being consistent when things are working well and especially if we are troubled, honors God in the greatest way. And because God is faithful and able to make all sufficiency abound in your life, the present afflictions are not to be compared to the glory and reward that will manifest if we continue to take God at His word.

Scripture encourages us to "Keep a praise on our lips and to speak the word." To have our hearts and spirits filled with expectancy just because God said so. Thus, eliminating and annulling unbelief that the adversary attempts to construct as a stronghold to keep you spiritually oppressed and barren.

The testimony of believers is more effective because of daily submission, coupled with patience to live the life set before us while we accept the cross assigned to our individual path. 'More easily said than done. Why? We have power to choose and we don't always function in good judgment.

In our arrogance, we are less committed to God through actions of self-promotion and intellectual prowess. It is inevitable to falter when decisions aren't made based on the word but our logic and feelings. Which is a recipe for spiritual disaster.

We must remember that every good gift come from above. "If you abide in him and his word abide in you, ask what you will and it shall be done."

Despite all the victories we've won through the help of the Holy Spirit, when fulfillment of promises are delayed many find themselves at the cross road of quitting. And you wonder why.

He is still the same God that granted every moment of happiness in the past, the identical God that delivered you from former strongholds. The same God that saved your soul. And he remains as is: "Omnipotent and steadfast in his love and care for his children."

Why do we doubt?

"When the cares of life take precedence over the word and daily commitment, our faith is choked." The entanglements of life, and elitist attitudes often arrayed as a badge of honor by some believers and lack of application of the word are bases for losing faith in God.

We hinder the flow of the Spirit from flourishing within us. *Preoccupation,* is a stealthy operation by the enemy to get you to believe you can manage without all the extras some Christians associate with living by faith. Such as, fasting, praying, tithing, and repenting consistently.

As a result of not yielding a matter to the guidance of the Holy Spirit, we of course are moved by our emotions and passions which are governed or controlled by our human frailty, and leads one to operate in the strength of their flesh. The battles we face are all spiritual, and must be won by the spirit of the WORD.

It is real to feel discouraged. And we all have moments when we have been discouraged. However, when discouragement is coupled with disobedience we develop the following:

➢ Governing thoughts contrary to God's word

➢ Limit our directional move in him

➢ Thwart the overflow of joy promised to them that dwell in his presence; and

➢ Create a vacuum for Satan to setup fortified strongholds in the mind, thus the portal from which flows unbelief that eventually saturates the heart or soul of mankind.

All converts are delivered from some form of darkness and habits that were displeasing in the eyes of God. As we grow in Grace and knowledge of our salvation, our understanding deepens when we cease leaning upon our limited understanding and just simply believe because God promised you.

We realize there isn't anything that we have to toil for according to our flesh because of the promise of transference – he promised to position his children in places of dominion and authority to take the spoil of the land. Remember the battle isn't physical and cannot be subdued by application of carnal methodologies.

He gives all things freely to them that believe and ask accordingly . . . practice tapping into his will. In addition to those who not only believe, but use their faith at his direction. Meaning, we give as we have been blessed, we are spiritually astute and watchful, we pray for all, especially our adversaries and never position ourselves to be conduits of evil as his children. And to conclude, we should expect every word to be fulfilled.

What prevents many Believers from entering such a flow of God's abundance where doubt is obliterated is unpreparedness. Many believe they are going to heaven without so much a thought given **who** heaven is prepared for. Prepared people. People who believe that God is.

Likewise, our preparation in life must consist of persistent faith in dark hours, when God seems quiet and without answers to your dilemma. It's during these moments we must persist and not return to formal dark practices; our hearts must render true to him in spirit in the face of pain, suffering and what feels like abandonment. We must be assured during these times of testing what is being produced will only equip you for the ascent and fulfillment of his promises.

When we skip talking to God and practice being in his presence for guidance and to receive his seal of approval for our undertakings, we force the blessings to be withheld. Our thinking is impeded, which governs our actions that produce the deeds that are not conducive to living in the flow of God's divine realm. Which must be lived by faith and in faith.

CHAPTER 3
No More Crumbs
Mt 15: 21-28

It is essential for us to have possessions because they are used to provide basic needs while we are on earth. (Naked I came… everything we have is a loan and will take nothing from this realm. So, we should learn to be effective managers of the trust.)

The Lord in His provision for us sees to it that we are made comfortable in every way. (Intercessor – Consoler – Advocate – Provider – Healer)

God wants life to be comfortable for us, but we must also learn to cope with those times when life is uncomfortable and inconvenient. Phil 4: 11-12 (NIV) I am not saying this because I am in need, for I have learned to be content whatever the circumstances. I know what it is to be in need, and I know what it is to have plenty. I have learned the secret of being content in any and every situation, whether well fed or hungry, whether living in plenty or in want.

Contentment is an essential part of our Christian growth and maturity; however, we cannot allow contentment to become containment. 2 Cor 9: 9-11 And God is able to make all grace abound toward you, that you, always having all sufficiency in all things, may have an abundance for every good work. As it is written: He has dispersed abroad, He has given to the poor, His righteousness endures forever. Now may He who supplies seed to the sower, and bread for food, supply and multiply the seed you have sown and increase the fruits of your righteousness, while you are enriched in everything for all liberality, which causes thanksgiving through us to God.

It is proven that the Lord loves us; however, our faith in Him will be tested. 1 Pet 1: 6-7 In this you greatly rejoice, though now for a little while, if need be, you have been grieved by various trials, that the genuineness of your faith, being much more precious than gold that perishes, though it is tested by fire, may be found to praise, honor, and glory at the revelation of Jesus Christ.

If we run from intimidation, we will always be crippled by other's opinions of us.

Too often we accept the lie of our circumstances over the truth of our position.

Anointing to royalty can never be earned; it is always imparted as a gift.

Rev 5: 9-10 (NIV) And they sang a new song: You are worthy to take the scroll and to open its seals, because You were slain, and with Your Blood You purchased men for God from every tribe and language and people and nation. You have made them to be a Kingdom and priests, to serve our God, and they will reign on the earth.

No matter how many times we may be denied, we must remain aggressive in achieving our heart's desires.

There will also be times when we will hear logical arguments as to why it is that we should just accept the present set of circumstances and not try any more.

Phil 3: 12 Not that I have already attained, or am already perfected; but I press on, that I may lay hold of that for which Christ Jesus has also laid hold of me.

Living off crumbs is only for a season; it will not be a permanent situation!

Many of us are about to experience radical changes in our life – from lack to plenty- from scarcity to abundance – and from crumbs to a feast! Amos 9: 13 (NIV) The days are coming, declares the Lord, when the reaper will be overtaken by the plowman and the planter by the one treading grapes. New wine will drip from the mountains and flow from all the hills.

Commentary:

When we experience a dark vortex, it speaks of life's fluctuations where what is familiar shifts; occasionally one is thrust into a dimension of abundance or lack, however, what is most paramount is first not to lose hope if so be it you find yourself on the down side of life. It is just a transition. To every believer is given the promise of divine provision as a covenant right wherefore, when reduction happens, we are encouraged to be patient, to look up or have a positive outlook on life.

To rest in the assurance of GOD as a loving Father and generous provider. Which include provision and protection; for he is well able to perform what he promised simply because it is impossible for God to lie and he delights in honoring those who have invested into the kingdom through usage one's time, talent and resources, which he multiplies or expands to bring natural and spiritual increase that sets us up for the next dimensional work and move of God in the earth through our lives.

In addition, our expansion in God also creates additional responsibility and care for those whom he assigns to our journey in specific seasons. We are reminded to remember ourselves having suffered affliction and having been comforted and to share liberally with those in bondage the depth of compassion and grace we have received. For we are interconnected and workmen together in Christ for the advancement of the kingdom; we help each other's growth or induce their demise.

Every person has ingrained in them a seed to flourish however, it cannot mature and become the original intent if we are shrouded in external opinions or lack courage to walk amid giants or face down naysayers and adhere to the written report of the LORD; we are healed, we are delivered, we are anointed or empowered with special power to soar.

We can demand return of stolen property, family and relations and rely on with rock-solid expectancy for the WORD to underwrite the cost. The thief when found must return seven-fold however, I am of the opinion if we ask in faith for God to super-size the return as a double portion he can do it just for the asking.

We must remain vigilant in our obtainment of every promise; every manifested promise is connected to a new season of joy, trials, fulfillment, and if we stand strong will increase trust and strengthen our position in God.

We learn to surround ourselves with likeminded positive individuals to flourish, where doors of significant opportunities open that leads to massive wealth, unlimited influence and dominion in the earth.

Just imagine having one great idea that impacts the entire world. This can only be realized when we understand and believe that we don't have to settle for the crumbs of life but in fact, can create the product or service that feeds the GLOBE.

CHAPTER 4
Perfecting Our Love Walk
1 Jn 4: 12-16

The way we presently live life in the world undoubtedly has its advantages as well as disadvantages.

What becomes increasingly difficult is being able to live in the world while refraining from having the world affect us. 1 Jn 4: 4-6 You are of God, little **children, and have overcome them, because He who is in you is greater than he who is in the world. They are of the world. Therefore, they speak as of the world, and the world hears them. We are of God. He who knows God hears us; he who is not of God does not hear us. By this we know the spirit of truth and the spirit of error.**

Commentary:

The art of perfecting love or growing mature in love requires emotional realization - it is essential for improving the quality of life, it's what we attain when we learn to get better at living by eliminating our eccentric behavior that's occasionally influenced by passive-aggression; and that includes loving folks just as they are. It must be settled and is foremost imperative to resolve you cannot force someone to change or accept your belief system; even if your position is right. The delicate balance Christians must develop is to show acceptance for the 'person' and not their behavior if a person's lifestyle is contrary to Scripture. Also, we are not called to be combative – mean-spirited and shun those with whom with disagree just because their worldview differs; you must be cognizant of the assignment. It is the mandate of Faith to love as you have been loved, which means we cannot be selective based on what we desire folks to be.

But, I am a Christian you say – so? Live like one, I say. You can't be a fisherman of souls when you are constantly scaring away the fish... sometimes, being stealthy and gentle is the best approach and can take you a long way in being of service for the Kingdom. Get rid of your plans... God doesn't need them. "For I know the plans I have for you, saith the Lord." And that includes how we should reach the world.

This very application of grace provides a platform for all without Christ to possibly come to him because in essence, he has said to us all 'don't try to change, you wouldn't know what to change, so just come as you are. I accept you just as you are...' and we too, must have the same mindset to love accordingly and gradually share the doctrine of our faith.

Some Christians are belligerent and lack patience with those who sit in darkness, forgetting their former state was equally the same. We weren't naturally born into the Kingdom – it took God some time to get your heart ready to accept him. He could have condemned all of us but what would that achieve? God's goal is to have a ready bride to meet his Son ... thus, our heavenly Father has nurtured and loved us through numerous offenses because he could see the end from the beginning. There is a bigger picture in view – Wherefore, we, Christians, must remember we are not called to condemned, we are called to WITNESS, PRAY, FAST AND GIVE.

In our quest to be relevant, we must be careful what we give up in lieu of taking a moral stand because we don't want to seem judgmental. Sadly, sometimes the messenger of Christ is tacky in presentation – I understand many do want to identify with this. But listen, we can't hide; we are the light and must rise to the occasion to shine. It's important to recognize the tactics of the adversary to shut you up-if Christians don't lift Christ in the marketplace, at the neighborhood salon, or boutiques and merely regurgitate prophecies and testimonies among Christians only on Sunday, how will humanity be drawn to him?

It is critical for the Kingdom to have earthly representation---every Christian is on assignment. As ambassadors or envoys, we cannot afford to demonstrate behavior that is less than stellar and spiritual towards those who are sinners; being professional would greatly make up for uncouthness when you don't feel spiritual. And sometimes, you won't but what is at stake is precious.

Of course, the play on words has made SIN, fashionable. From the highest authority in the land, the White House, to scared halls where the tenets of faith should be preached in truth, we see spiritual erosion led by an errant spirit that operates through the conveyance of smooth words, but in truth, are twisted lies and damnable doctrines that are an affront to God.

Surely, we feel that we should defend God – God doesn't need defending. He needs to be represented.

But don't be fool, there is nothing chic about living in sin. Regardless who the messenger is, we are all '*fleeting* personalities' that will give account to God.

The reality is sin is sometimes fun that's why many intentionally waddle, but never underestimate the sting that is just waiting to hit you; a blow of eternal separation from God if you aren't fortunate enough to surrender in time.

Notwithstanding, the shift in the culture can cause anger, frustration, and a desire for separation from our fellowman, but to do that is the antithesis of what the Lord sent us to do.

Whereas we understand some may feel frustrated and inept who were born during a certain period, especially prior to the technological explosion of personal computers and the internet in the home; indulgence in chat rooms, and dating sites etc., created a subculture that is now with more prominence and influence than the outreach of many churches.

And so many folks have not caught up and perhaps understand the shaping of ideologies produced by the tech-boom has deeply affected modern-day society. But the world is, and yes, Christians included, different.

Silicon Valley made its way across millions of thresholds and there is no stopping – those who are not prepared simply must open yourself to learn so that your Christian walk can be effective – the bombardment has been overwhelming for so many, yet, all so common for those born prior to 1980 and just preaching within four walls or merely attending religious services will not make the biggest difference. The way people indulge in sin has mutated – if you are going to represent the Kingdom on earth, you too, must learn what the Spirit is first saying, and then make yourself your available, and learn how to be strategic in your presentation in the marketplace.

The Kingdom of God must have prepared minds – Christians must be RELEVANT. The church age is still holding hostage those who gave their hearts to Christ by functioning in antiquated practices --- we can't thrive in this world if we are still being fed weak doctrine that does not challenge you to grow and position yourself to impact your sphere of the world.

While the Church slept, the enemy sowed tares in the midst... our slumber cannot be eradicated through anger, we will only take back lost territory through the authority of the Word, but we must function with grace and kindness.

As much as we would like to lay the burden for the deprivation of our culture upon the shoulders of the world we must examine our thinking and realize that it's really not their fault. 2 Chr 7: 14 If My people; --- Prov 11: 10-11 When it goes well with the righteous, the city rejoices; and when the wicked perish, there is jubilation. By the blessing of the upright the city is exalted, but it is overthrown by the mouth of the wicked. ------ READ GEN 18: 20-32

For Believers, we are never without a word to direct us from the Lord – a Rhema word that gives life and refreshes a parched soul. Amid this very noisy environment (world) with many opposing views and thousands who are spiritually lawless, we have a responsibility to demonstrate the love of God by extending through kindness and not force, the life-changing word of the gospel, which can be bring about the change we desire to see in our loved ones and possibly in your opposition.

One of our greatest issues is to be able to separate a person's behavior from who they are; acceptance doesn't mean approval. Rom 15: 7 Therefore receive one another, just as Christ also received us, to the glory of God.

Another challenge is whether we should speak the truth to someone that we know is demonstrating destructive behavior. Prov 17: 17 A friend loves always, and a brother is born for adversity.

Our heavenly Father wants us to know that the people around us should not be enamored by our gifts but by our love. Jn 13: 34-35 A new commandment I give to you, that you love one another; as I have loved you, that you also love one another. By this all will know that you are My disciples, if you have love for one another.

It must be fully understood that nothing else in the Kingdom works without love being at the center of it. Gal 5: 6 For in Christ Jesus neither circumcision nor uncircumcision avails anything, but faith working through love. ----- 1 Cor 13: 1-3 Though I speak with the tongues of men and of angels, but if I have not love, I have become sounding brass or a clanging cymbal. And though I have the gift of prophecy, and understand all mysteries and all knowledge, and though I have all faith, so that I could remove mountains, but have not love, I am nothing. And though I bestow all my goods to feed the poor, and though I give my body to be burned, but have not love, it profits me nothing!

It becomes easier for Believers to navigate life when you take in consideration as denoted in I John 4:12-6 – we are set in a construct that is designed to ignore us based on who God is within. Our role as ambassadors is to share and live kingdom principles as best as is humanly possible. Never should one concede or be deceived in thinking that the relevance of the Church and being compassionate is outdated; we hold fast to truth that is self-evident and in operation in the earth through them that believe and will continue to perfect the things that concerns us daily as we make ourselves submissive to God's care.

To be truly pleasing to God it requires coupling of your faith with submission of your will to reflect him by becoming a willing vessel who walks in love.

IMPORTANCE

CHAPTER 5
The Importance of a Father Prov 17: 6

Many men have had to endure the void and emptiness of not knowing a father's love or input in their life.

It is a man's father that ultimately validates when a young man has become a man. Gen 49: 1-2 And Jacob called his sons and said, gather together, that I may tell you what shall befall you in the last days: gather together and hear, you sons of Jacob, and listen to Israel you father.

The absence of a father's involvement in a child's life leaves them imbalanced. Prov 4: 1-2 Hear my children, the instruction of a father, and give attention to know understanding; for I give you good doctrine; do not forsake my law.

Women physically create a bond with their children before they ever enter the world; men have to create a relationship.

Fathers must be careful how they live their lives, what they do can affect their children's development. Ps 78: 5-8 For He established a testimony in Jacob, and appointed a law in Israel, which He commanded our fathers, that they should make them known to their children; that the generation to come might know them, the children who would be born, that they may arise and declare them to their children, that they may set their hope in God, and not forget the works of God, but keep His commandments; and may not be like their fathers, a stubborn and rebellious generation, a generation that did not set its heart aright, and whose spirit was not faithful to God.

We are presently living in a fatherless generation, but that trend cannot continue. Prov 29: 15 The rod and rebuke give wisdom, but a child left to himself brings shame to his mother.

The critical part of a father's responsibility is to provide a solid spiritual foundation for his children. Gen 18: 17-19 And the Lord said: Shall I hide from Abraham what I am doing, since Abraham shall surely become a great and mighty nation, and all the nations of the earth shall be blessed in him? For I have known him, in order that he may command his children and his household after him, that they keep the way of the Lord, to do righteousness and justice, that the Lord may bring to Abraham what He has spoken to him.

Our children may not want to hear it, but we must protect them from the elements of life that we know will destroy them. Ps 22: 19-21 But You, O Lord, do not be far from me; O my strength, hasten to help me! Deliver me from the sword; my precious life from the power of the dog! Save me from the lion's mouth and from the horns of the wild oxen!

A child's basic concept of what God is like should be based upon their relationship with their father. 1 Cor 4: 15-16 (NIV) Apostle Paul said, "Even though you have ten thousand guardians in Christ, you do not have many fathers, for in Christ Jesus I became your father through the gospel. Therefore, I urge you to imitate me."

Fatherhood reaches far beyond one night when the moon was bright and the mood was right --- it is serious ministry!

Commentary:

Importance of a Father

We have a dichotomy of two significant truths relating to the value of what a father brings to the family structure: in the spiritual, God, our heavenly father proactively works through the Holy Spirit to provide guidance, direction, and protection in accord with his word for his children to live in divine alignment and original intent. Where we are productive, proactive and examples to the world as a paradigm of achievement and expanding more in the spiritual, emotional and physical realms of life…

Likewise, a natural father establishes an atmosphere in the home where his spouse and children have assurance of his protection and love, and leads the family on a trajectory that always produces wellness and empowers the unit to become productive in every facet of the family dynamic.

Our heavenly father instructs the family (the body of Christ), to establish a position or posture of remembering who he is and what he has done to deter the chances of imposters infiltrating the family that would contaminate the lineage with idol worship, riotous living, debauchery and related offenses.

A natural father takes similarly the same position when comes to the intrusion of his family construct; a good father would gauge his family's interaction with outsiders, offer advice and admonish whom to remove from their social circles and remind them of the importance of sticking together and caring for one another. Just as God through Jesus Christ exemplified his care for humanity and those who chose to answer the call to live for him and dwell in the family.

There is something so dynamic about a father who is balanced in mind, spirit, and soul – he causes his family to flourish and enjoy their development. Just as God who laughs with us, and at us, perhaps frowns at our disbelief when we decide to leave the protective arc of his safety, allowing impostures to infiltrate our spirit that influences deeds that are affront to His nature. One of many positive facets of having the presence of a father is first to establish relevance or identity. God made it known by calling us sons and daughters of God.

Secondly, fathers must admonish. The word *admonish* means "to warn." Apostle Paul needed to warn the Children of Israel that their pride and arrogance was only going to hurt them and the church. If not checked, it would result in schisms in the body of Christ.

A father encourages his children. He may exhort his son to keep his room clean, use proper manners in the presence of guests, or show politeness toward adults. Likewise, we need to exhort our spiritual children in things like trusting God, to be contrite of sin, obey the Word, to utilize their spiritual gifts, to have a servant heart, forgiving those that have wronged them, tenacious in difficulty, consistent in prayer, to pray without ceasing, study the Word, share their faith, and give to the least of them. We need to know others well enough that our exhortations flow naturally from a heart of love for their spiritual welfare and progress.

With so many children suffering with identity crisis a good father sets the example. Often time children begin to imitate what they see their fathers do. Therefore, it is imperative for fathers to have soberness of mind, you are directly influencing the mindset of the next generation.

A Spiritual Father Disciplines His Children: 4:18-21

Shall I come to you with a rod or with love and a spirit of gentleness? Paul identified a group of proud, arrogant, conflict-ridden believers in Corinth. Akin to all children, whether spiritual or natural, the group felt safe to be contrary because the "Father" (Paul) was away.

He sent word to inform of his return; Paul wants them to know they are greatly mistaken! He is coming to them soon, if the Lord wills, and when he does he will find out if there is any divine power behind all their words. He would not hesitate to rebuke, or administer church discipline if necessary.

When spiritual children refuse to adhere to sound doctrine fathers must administer church discipline as a witness against their deeds. Not to shame or repel from the faith but, to bring correction and restoration.

Mt. 18:15-17

We need to make up our minds that we love our spiritual children more than we love our own comfort.

Taking responsibility

CHAPTER 6
The Responsibility of Leadership
Num 18: 6-7

Being a leader in the 21st century requires a lot more than in days gone by.

No one can be an effective leader without having a proper worldview. Prov 27: 23-24 Be diligent to know the state of your flocks, and attend to your herds; for riches are not forever, nor does a crown endure to all generations.

Present attitudes toward church have produced a people that too often see the greater responsibility for the care of God's people as being the concern of one person.

Not always will core leaders approve of the tactics and methods used by the visionary, however, you must believe in the vision and agree with where we are headed.

There are five qualities that every leader should possess:

1) A leader must be STRONG = they should be a person who can take both instruction and criticism without being offended. It is relative to a person holding a ladder; the person climbing the ladder must have the confidence

that the one holding the ladder is competent and won't wilt when given instruction.

2) A leader must be ATTENTIVE = they must be alert and always paying attention; able to pick up things quickly. Attentive people don't have to be chased after, they understand the first time.

3) A leader has the quality of FAITHFULNESS = this is not about being faithful to God but faithful to their leader. There must be faith in and commitment to their leader. These types of people can always be found holding the ladder. These people don't always need praise to keep going.

4) A leader needs the quality of FIRMNESS = these are people that are not exploited by manipulative people. Terrorism is not new --- people in church have been doing it for a long time and their purpose is control and destruction. It is usually hidden in language that seems every bit right but slanted.

5) A leader must possess the quality of LOYALTY = this does not mean that they will agree all the time. You may disagree with the leader's head but should not have to question their heart. You may disagree with how the

leader does things but not why they are done a certain way. You may disagree with the leader's methods but not their motivations. 1 Sam 14: 6-7 Then Jonathan said to the young man who bore his armor: 'Come, let us go over to the garrison of these uncircumcised; it may be that the Lord will work for us. For nothing restrains the Lord from saving by many or by few.' So, his armor bearer said to him; 'Do all that is in your heart. Go then, here I am with you, according to your heart.'

There are three principles that we should learn to follow: if we disagree with our leader we don't do it publicly. It should be discussed with that person in private.

If we disagree, we ought to search our motives before we speak. Some people are afraid to speak up and will pump someone else up to do it for them. If we disagree, we should be sure we don't do it for personal gain.

Commentary:

The styles of Leadership in the church will vary based on education, economics, travel, socialization, political views, and so forth. As well as establish preferences regarding the genre of music, hour of worship, community involvement and missions. Notwithstanding, the etymology of the word 'lead,' 'leaders,' and 'leadership,' share as their common root word 'to go.' Effective leadership function within the framework of family-care where the center, or church, is first nurtured, then the offspring is reared, equipped, challenged, and inspired to go out and impact nations.

America as a shining example of leadership in so many disciplines and industries, but must also increase its influence within western ministries; sadly, many with the capacity to influence have not stepped up to the plate to lead a national campaign – some are not open to share the platform by which many could be helped. Ministries, and leadership in general must become a part of the global commentary and shift its focus toward global influence. According to Scripture, to have a worldview has always been at the heart of God --- to go into all the world (where ever God assigns) is essential; the calling was never relegated only to religious services.

"Whatever your hands find to do, do it with all your might." The shift in our priorities created a vacuum. We have allowed a spiritual vacuum by default by not opposing secular ideologies that are in clear violation of scripture, thus, sustaining a stronghold that we must contend with on a global scale. Leadership cannot remain quiet... part of its responsibility is to speak truth to power and those without voice need representation from GOD. In addition, leaders must be adaptive and capable of learning as they lead; ethically, practically, faithfully and must be givers.

In support of Scripture Proverbs 27:23-24 – Leadership must know how to delegate responsibilities to managers (those in leadership position) to achieve efficacy in operations, yet, leaders as all CEO's must personally assess their data (conferences, measurements from workshops, and training programs) to ascertain the wellness of their parishioners. Not every program is a good one. And whatever recommendations are made for change, ultimately the decision comes from the top down, you can't pass off making tough decisions. Also, a leader must make oneself available but is not exclusively assigned to handle every concern and should know the difference between when they are managing and leading. Effective leaders give room … those who serve in leadership must understand there is a collective responsibility in doing God's work.

Leaders as it has been written "constantly seek to exchange their knowledge because that's how we increase our leadership skills." Subsequently, the struggle within some ministries is the eroding ideology that the leadership path is predicated upon votes or personal consensus; it is not uncommon for core leaders and parishioners not to fully grasp everything a leader desires to do. Nevertheless, there is a correct way to handle disagreements to prevent discord. In the event of disconnect, smart leaders are good listeners and recognizes sound advice; they also know when to step back and wait.

Leadership encompasses having conviction and courage to apply models that shifts and stimulate consciousness, and create awareness of individual responsibility to self, community and the vision of the work; this enables core leaders and co-laborers within a ministry to utilize their skillset to augment the vision.

Sadly, in some black and Hispanic congregations, the philosophy of pastoral availability becomes a sticky issue; culturally for many decades some pastors adopted an open-door policy where folks, members or not, could just come without parameters. Not only is this disruptive, but enforced an ideology that's not supported in Scripture, and induced many unproductive practices within those ministries where some are illegal.

To be specific, many of those spiritual leaders wanting to be a 'good leader' would often engage in areas of expertise and training for which they had none i.e., psychology, sociology, financial management, even sharing medical advice; although in the spirit of wanting to meet the needs of the people but clearly very few were educated and trained in these capacities and yes, were also illegal for them to do so. Financial advisers, medical professionals, lawyers, and any other restricted professions requires certification and preaching the gospel doesn't exempt one from becoming a legal practitioner.

As part of understanding the five qualities leaders must possess, knowing when not to over apply one's self is critical; leadership through the leading of the Holy Spirit understand the power of "Words." And "Words build the architecture of our thoughts and paint images in the mind. Like dance and music, they can alter how and what we think about and, as such, are some of the most powerful tools of leadership." All who seek leadership positions should be prepared to serve…there is no honor without first humility.

Revelation

CHAPTER 7
The Revelation of The Church
Mt. 16: 13-19

From century to century the church has undergone many transitions; however, this present generation finds itself without a spiritual identity.

This present generation and dispensation requires a radical church that is both potent and relevant. Acts 5: 12-16 And through the hands of the apostles many signs and wonders were done among the people. And they were all with one accord in Solomon's porch. Yet none of the rest dared join them, but the people esteemed them highly. And believers were increasingly added to the Lord, multitudes of both men and women, so that they brought the sick out into the streets and laid them on beds and couches, that at least the shadow of Peter passing by might fall on some of them.

Also, a multitude gathered from the surrounding cities to Jerusalem, bringing sick people and those who were tormented by unclean spirits, and they were all healed.

The establishment of the church brought into existence an entity that would enforce the mandates of the Kingdom of God while God ruled sovereignly from heaven.

It is the devil's desire to neutralize the church in any way possible. Mt. 5: 13-16 You are the salt of the earth; but if the salt loses its flavor, how shall it be seasoned? It is then good for nothing but to be thrown out and trampled underfoot by men. You are the light of the world. A city that is set on a hill cannot be hidden. Nor do they light a lamp and put it under a basket, but on a lampstand, and it gives light to all that are in the house. Let your light so shine, etc.

Our greatest problem is that we attempt to sustain God's church with our life, while in eternity the Lord God desired to have a church that was completely filled with the life of Christ.

In the Lord's eyes the church has two positions; as to her life, the church is the Body of Christ, but regarding her future, she is the bride of Christ. --- As the Body of Christ we are to manifest the life of Christ.

It must be understood that Christ's death was more than a sacrifice for sin, but He died for the church because of love. Eph. 5:25 Husbands love your wives, etc.

There is a revelation of the church that every believer must possess; and that is, that we are being prepared to become the Bride of Christ. Eph. 5: 26-27 That He might sanctify and cleanse her with the washing of water by the word, that He might present her to Himself a glorious church, not having spot or wrinkle or any such thing, but that she should be holy and without blemish.

The Word of God has not become "Rhema" until we allow it to illuminate and expose those areas in our life that are not like Christ.

Demonic forces cannot prevail against a church that is filled with the light and life of Christ!

Commentary:

Having an encounter with God through the Holy Spirit brings to every believer exposure into a dimension that cannot be understood by human intellect, and gives a tactical advantage to address and subdue conflict, as well as inspire participation in bringing transformation in the earth through one's *involvement* in service. We become miracle workers thus, fulfilling scripture where Christ declared "Greater works will you do if you believe and abide in me."

Another revelation of this subject is God's desire to equip every believer with knowledge of God's purpose for sending his Son to gather creation back into his presence, and validates the identity of the Church as being chosen and set apart for a specific purpose. This points to preselection and places significant value upon each person.

- There is a unique understanding the Spirit gives in its reference to the body as a "City of Light."

- We should be encouraged to take the gifts and talents entrusted to our care to honor him in the marketplace, where God is glorified through the implementation thereof.

As a city of redeemed people, we are admonished to take what level of comfort we have received and share liberally with the downtrodden; those afflicted physically and emotional. To love the unloved and *persona non-grata* (the outcast) in society.

In addition to be a "city of redemption" (a haven where the hurting can resort for instruction and prayer); to be a witness in all the world as we share the love of God that was shed abroad in our hearts and live as envoys of peace in the earth.

Unfortunately, in our advanced academic culture, the continuum of thought is that only a knowledge-based society that is mastering the philosophy of lives past, and those disciplined in *advanced-studies* of best-living practices, possibly trained in six-sigma with a rank associated to it, reflect the supreme arena where human consciousness thrives best. And in this community of thought, demonstration of intellectual prowess is where humanity is capable of making its own decisions that are relevant in accord with the times, and need not consult outside of an individual's power to choose his or her own path.

Sadly, many ascribe that there is no need for this one called "God." In their eyes, only the weak and unlearned are losers in need of religion as the crutch upon which they are upheld. Established religions exact too much from their leisure and world view of life.

Many churches and other religious institutions have etched out the purpose of the Holy Spirit to bring believers revelation, guidance and inspire conviction to grow. In our pious society, many deem being consecrated to God as an ancient practice without having any modern-day relevance.

The measurement that permeates is a people who may have a heart for God in theory, but in relations, do not know him because there is no application of the word in deed. "Faith without works is invalid." If we say we love him there must be manifestation on multiple levels;

first, personal. Second, we must demonstrate our love and commitment in the way we interact with others; to love our neighbor as we love ourselves. Third, we must witness. The latter is the present threat and target of the adversary to obliterate by diminishing religious freedom and expression of one's faith through drafted legislation.

The secular position is, "Believe what you will but keep it to yourself." We don't need to know. This ideology is in direct conflict with the purpose of the Church as ordained by God to go into all the world and proclaim the good news.

To fully grasp why there is a struggle one must concede that receiving revelation of the unseen is not easy. Most Christians find the symbolism of the cross easier to accept than the manifestation of Pentecost (being filled with the spirit). Why? In the minds of some the wooden cross is a tangible object whereas the Holy Spirit is not.

When there is no identity with deeper spiritual things we see the expression of secularism incorporated in what should be sacred. Why? Lack of revelation of the purpose of the Church.

Higher education proclaims if one's life is to be rewarding and filled with limitless opportunities you must matriculate at certain universities however, with all the learning in the world we cannot dodge one small but pertinent fact, we are not our own. Psalm 24 The opening line is "The earth is the Lord's, and the fullness **thereof**; the world, and they that dwell therein".

We belong to a family. God's children aren't nomads..." We are God's workmanship established in Christ Jesus before the foundation of time" and assigned to manifest good works, which implies the life of believers should be productive and innovative. We are not to linger or return to old unprofitable mannerisms that alienates us from being intimately interwoven to God's plan. No much we increase in learning, occasionally, we lack understanding of why we are here when our personal engagement with God is not based on learning the purpose of His will for your life. God is not merely interested in hearing about our woes, he is concerned about the total person, and that entails our development to become conduits of change in the earth. Where each-one, reach-one.

The Holy Spirit leads us into the realm of the supernatural to behold mysteries and do what the carnal cannot achieve. Where many are disenchanted and lose heart but, we through the revelation of who we are become embolden to take territory occupied by our spiritual adversary.

We learn to get comfortable being uncomfortable because the battle is not ours. And the exploits others dream of doing but are unable, we beam with confidence and assurance to go beyond the norm.

At the end of the day, what God is doing through the establishment of the Church (not brick and mortar) but the Holy Spirit, is preparing His people for the return of His son, to present him a bride that is without blemish. A bride that is strong and ready.

We are setup to return. Wherefore, let us put aside every weight and sin that easily entraps and press for the higher call of God in Christ Jesus.

You may be the first person in your family in generations to come to know Christ and lack support to be more effective in your witness, we shouldn't lose heart but ask for what is needed. "I am sure of this, that he who began a good work in you will bring it to completion at the day of Jesus Christ." *Philippians 1:6*

Throughout history we see the neglect of the Church; the abandonment of faith and shifting priorities, but it is the one institution that is needed and have stood the test of time.

"Purpose to know the will of God for your life through the revealing power of the Holy Spirit – there is no experience akin to it. No comparison in any sphere of life."

The True Source

CHAPTER 8
The True Source of Strength
Eph 3: 14-19

It is evident by the course of natural events that prevail in the earth from *day-to-day*, the body of Christ has yet to understand the totality of her being. Jn 9: 39-41 And Jesus said: For judgment, I have come into this world, that those who do not see may see, and that those who see may be made blind. Then some of the Pharisees who were with Him heard these words, and said to Him; are we blind also? Jesus said to them, "If you were blind, you would have no sin; but now you say, we see. Therefore, your sin remains."

Even if we don't want to, the enemy of our soul wants to fight and we must be prepared to fight back. Lk 22: 31-32 And the Lord said: Simon, Simon! Indeed, Satan has asked for you, that he may sift you as wheat. But I have prayed for you, that your faith should not fail; and when you have returned to Me, strengthen your brethren.

Our ability to resist the enemy depends on the depth of our relationship which supplies us with inner power. 2 Cor 3: 5-6 Not that we are sufficient of ourselves to think of anything as being from ourselves, but our sufficiency is from God, who also made us sufficient as ministers of the new covenant, not of the letter but of the Spirit; for the letter kills, but the Spirit gives life.

We must be stout hearted, strong for service, strong for suffering and strong for fighting.

2 Cor 12: 7-10 And lest I should be exalted by the abundance of the revelations, a thorn in the flesh was given to me, a messenger of Satan to buffet me, lest I be exalted above measure. Concerning this thing I pleaded with the Lord three times that it might depart from me. And He said to me; My grace is sufficient for you, for My strength is made perfect in weakness. Therefore, most gladly I will rather boast in my infirmities, that the power of Christ may rest upon me. Therefore, I take pleasure in infirmities, in reproaches, in needs, in persecutions, in distresses, for Christ's sake. For when I am weak, then I am strong. Stout - hearted = brave and resolute, dauntless

Commentary:

The summation of life can be said in one sentence ,"In him we move, live and have our being, and without him we can do nothing."

Our dependence upon God is primary; there is no other life giving source that can extend our days or give insight to mysteries that equips mankind to do exploits whereby millions are helped, and remove spiritual blindness that enables us to fellowship spirit-to-spirit. We would all stumble in darkness if it were not for God's desire to have relationship with humanity, which supersedes any notion that we are self-sufficient. We need him.

When we are enraged in spiritual warfare the weapons at our disposal to deploy are superior in every way not just to dismantle, but destroy the actual intent of the devil and prevent him from bringing disruption and instability.

As in Luke 22:31-32 – the plot of Satan is still to break us down but the only reason we are able to withstand is because of the early prayer prayed for all mankind – Jesus asked for our covering even before going to the cross. Which accentuates our responsbility to increase our consciousness and dependency that a force beyond human understanding fought for us and won.

We are not our own. We were bought with a price that no man could pay.

Sadly, many do not know that from the onset of human existence the struggle has always been about what God originally purposed; for we are his workmanship created in Christ Jesus to perform good works and to walk therein. And Satan's determination has always been to attempt to derail, destroy and forever annihilate many from the presence of God. The very realm that he will never again enjoy, but we can be restored even when we fall short; the plan of God includes our redemption and restoration (back to wholeness and right standing) because of the bigger purpose. And that purpose is what Satan hates...thus, we are the object of his fury.

Every Believer should boast – I am redeemed and can hear the spirit speak in the still of night that brings comfort when my soul is in agony. Whereas, Satan is sealed for destruction and knows it, Believers are daily beckoned to come closer and fortify themselves in the presence of God and guaranteed his protection and guidance.

Wherefore should be encouraged to share the depth of mercy we have received with those who fall before us, restoring them in the spirit of meekness considering ourselves. We are still standing only because God willed it so – our position should always be from a position of strength and confidence knowing that what God started he will complete.

A common strategy of the dark world is to offer us those things that have been identified as temptations that one may possibly yield to. Js 1: 12-15 Blessed is the man who endures temptation; for when he has been approved, he will receive the crown of life which the Lord has promised to those who love Him. Let no one say when he is tempted, God tempts me; for God, cannot be tempted by evil, nor does He Himself tempt anyone. But each one is tempted when he is drawn away by his own desires and enticed. Then, when desire has conceived, it gives birth to sin; and sin, when it is full – grown, brings forth death.

There should be a level of spiritual maturity that one ascribes to reach, settling that nothing will ever satisfy your soul, like the presence of God. And discourage being half committed and pledge our allegiance to a loving God. We owe him everything and nothing should compare to who he is and what he has done individually in the life of the believer.

It is never our ability that is in question; it is the brevity of our capacity! Capacity = the maximum amount or number that can be received or contained. Eph 4: 16 From Him the whole body, joined and held together by every supporting ligament, grows and builds itself up in love, as each part does its work.

When Mary Shows Up

CHAPTER 9
When Mary Shows Up
Lk 1: 39-45

There is a unique, specific, and divine intention that the Lord has for every one of us deposited into the earth realm. Eph 1: 3-6 Blessed be the God and Father of our Lord Jesus Christ, who has blessed us with every spiritual blessing in the heavenly places in Christ, just as He chose us in Him before the foundation of the world, that we should be holy and without blame before Him in love, having predestined us to adoption as sons by Jesus Christ to Himself, according to the good pleasure of His will, to the praise of the glory of His grace, by which He made us accepted in the Beloved.

Our progress and evolution in Christ will be determined by the level of fear that we allow in our lives. Gen 3: 9-10 Then the Lord God called to Adam and said to him; Where are you? So, he said, I heard Your voice in the garden, and I was afraid because I was naked, and I hid myself.

Our faith provides us with the ability to transcend time; however, God assigns a certain procedure and timing to the various stations of our life. Eccl 8: 5-6 (NIV) Whoever obeys His command will come to no harm, and the wise heart will know the proper time and procedure.

For there is a proper time and procedure for every matter, though a person may be weighed down by misery.

The conception of Jesus is truly supernatural, yet, at the same time it speaks to our involvement of what the Lord wants to do in the earth. READ LK 1: 28-38

It is imperative that we pay strict attention to every conversation that we have with the Lord because everything He wants us to do may not necessarily be spelled out. READ LK 1: 36 & 39

1 Cor 2: 14 But the natural man does not receive the things of the Spirit of God, for they are foolishness to him; nor can he know them, because they are spiritually discerned.

At some point, we all need the aid of someone that is assigned to come along side of us, and just the sound of their voice brings inspiration and hope. (TEXT V41) 2 Sam 16: 23 Now the advice of Ahithophel, which he gave in those days, was as if one had inquired at the oracle of God. So was all the advice of Ahithophel both with David and with Absalom.

There are times in our life when we need someone to help awaken dead places and purpose within us.

Even though there are instances of apparent delay we should always rest assured that the Lord's word to us is sure. Lk 1: 11-16 Then an angel of the Lord appeared to him, standing on the right side of the altar of incense. And when Zacharias saw him, he was troubled, and fear fell upon him. But the angel said to him: Do not be afraid, Zacharias, for your prayer is heard, and your wife Elizabeth will bear you a son and you will call his name John. (Jehovah has been gracious) And you will have joy and gladness, and many will rejoice at his birth. For he will be great in the sight of the Lord, and shall drink neither wine nor strong drink. He will also be filled with the Holy Spirit, even from his mother's womb. And he will turn many of the children of Israel to the Lord their God.

The understanding of the will of God and the power of God in our lives carries us to another dimension. Job 28: 12-13 But where can wisdom be found? And where is the place of understanding? Man, does not know its value, nor is it found in the land of the living.

It is very difficult to make a commitment to something that you don't have a true conviction about. Rom 8: 38-39 For I am persuaded that neither death nor life, nor angels nor principalities nor powers, nor things present nor things to come, nor height nor depth, nor any other created thing, shall be able to separate us from the love of God which is in Christ Jesus our Lord. --- Conviction = a fixed or firm belief

Commentary:

Every person needs to have a Mary encounter, where your spirit and desire is quickened – where you remember the passion to live your best life.

It is extremely easy to be inundated with noise from external voices that will cloud your judgment and dampen your drive to move forward wherefore, it speaks volumes of the necessity to connect with forward thinking people: those who see the future full of promise versus those with consistent negative reports.

Notwithstanding, it is imperative for everyone to accept his or her responsibility to first recognize when your connector shows up by being sensitive to the spirit, then, be humble enough to glean because we all aide in another's person development.

As we seek the will of God, one thing we must keep at the forefront is, he always gives a seed. No matter what the endeavor is, you will always be given a seed that could materialize to something greater. However, this is only realized when we are faithful with what we have... The word over your life cannot yield unfruitful if you stay connected to the Source. There is no hardship or setback that can annul God's promise to deliver your vision to full-term if you consistently put him first; He is more than ecstatic to give what he has promised but will we condition ourselves for the journey?

Remember, anybody can start – startups take place every day but how many take time to equip and condition themselves for the down moments when no one is buying your products or services, church attendance is bleak, tithing and offerings are dwindling... how you proceed in faith is critical.

Of course, it goes without saying but bears mentioning this when many turn to devices of the past; old habits and thoughts speak loudly, which is equivalent to the children Israel wanting to turn back to Egypt while in the desert.

There is nothing worth returning to from your past – that's why God delivered you in the first place.

About Apostle Gilbert Coleman, Jr.

Apostle Coleman is the Senior Pastor of Freedom Christian Bible Fellowship in Philadelphia, Pennsylvania, and the presiding Bishop over Freedom Worldwide Covenant Ministries. God has given this man a 'burden' for men. It is his desire to see men come back to their God-given place as leaders in their homes, in their communities and in the house of God. The Transforming the Minds of Men Ministry is the vehicle through which the Lord has chosen to bring this vision to pass.

Apostle Coleman has also been blessed to shepherd other churches both nationally and internationally. Currently, there are eleven churches in the United States under the Freedom banner and others have been planted in Burundi, Ghana, India, Malawi, Nigeria, the Philippines, and Zimbabwe.

He is married to Deborah A. Coleman and is the proud father of three sons, one daughter and five grandchildren.

Dr. Gilbert Coleman
Transforming The Minds Of Men
6100 W Columbia Ave
Philadelphia Pa 19151
215-477-0800
Email - gcapostle9@gmail.com
Website - ttmomministries.org

Made in the USA
Charleston, SC
19 January 2017